INTRODUCTION

LOOK AT YOUR BODY! You are a complex machine, forever on the move, always going from place to place and never staying still – even if you were to sit motionless! How is your body able to keep up with all the things you want to do? Where does all the energy come from to jump about, take part in sports and do all the other things you do every single day? The answer lies inside you. Sitting within your chest are two large sponge-like organs called the lungs. Every time you take a breath, they fill with air from which your body takes an important gas known as oxygen. This gas is vital for life. It is involved in getting energy from the food you eat. This energy is what keeps you going. However your lungs are fragile objects, and from time to time need special protection to stop them coming into contact with harmful things.

The STUFF OF LIFE

LIFE DEPENDS on two "elements". One of these is energy. Living things need continuing supplies of energy to grow, move and carry out the thousands of chemical processes inside their bodies which keep them "alive". Plants use sunlight to get energy, and animals get it from food.

To make the energy available for life processes, both plants and animals need the second "element" – oxygen. Nearly all living things need to take in oxygen, to survive. They obtain it using a variety of body parts such as lungs, gills or networks of air tubes.

Sunlight

Carbon dioxide

Oxygen

SOLAR POWER
Plants use sunlight to get energy, in a process called photosynthesis. The substance which makes leaves green, called chlorophyll, traps light energy. The plant uses this to change carbon dioxide, which it takes from the air, and water from its roots, into sugar and oxygen, which the plant then gives off (above). The plant "burns" the sugar along with oxygen from the air, in a process called respiration. This releases energy which the plant can use to live and grow.

Water

MICRO-ORGANISMS
Like larger living things, most micro-organisms – such as a pond-dwelling amoeba (right) – require oxygen. These microbes have no active way of taking in oxygen. Instead, the gas seeps, or diffuses, through their thin body walls, to reach all of their body parts.

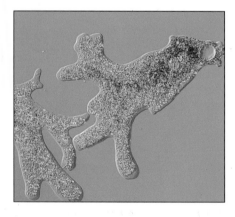

INSECTS
Many small creatures, like insects (left), have tubes inside their bodies to carry oxygen-containing air to their internal organs. These tubes open at holes that run along the insect's side, known as spiracles.

Spiracles

DEEP BREATHS
Some creatures in water have lungs and breathe air, like you do. They include mammals such as dolphins and whales. These mammals breathe through blowholes positioned on top of their heads. They have to surface regularly in order to take breaths of air, otherwise they would drown.

AIR AND ATMOSPHERE
The blanket of air around the Earth, the atmosphere, extends about 100 km (60 miles) up into space. It's composed of a mixture of gases, mainly nitrogen and also oxygen that is so important for life (see page 22).

BREATHING UNDERWATER
Creatures that live totally in water, like fish and starfish, "breathe" the oxygen that is dissolved in the water around them. Fish have feather-like gills that are filled with blood (below). These do the same job as the lungs of an air-breathing land animal. As water flows over them, oxygen is absorbed through their gills and into the fish's blood.

Air goes in and out through blowhole

Gills

Water out

Water in

AIR IN WATER
Humans are typical mammals, breathing air into their lungs to obtain the oxygen. They can stay underwater for long periods by breathing a supply of oxygen they have taken with them, in a back-tank or aqualung.

ENERGY NEEDS
The complex chemical processes inside a living thing are called its metabolism and energy is needed to drive them. Small creatures, such as shrews, have a fast metabolism and need a lot of energy for their body size. Larger animals, like elephants, need less energy for their size. Humans, like you, fall somewhere in between (right).

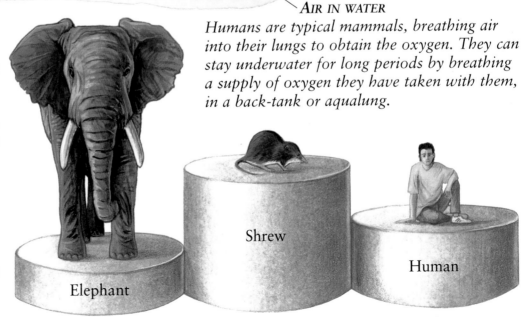

Shrew

Human

Elephant

The RESPIRATORY SYSTEM

THE PARTS OF A LIVING thing which obtain the vital supplies of oxygen from the surroundings are called the respiratory system. In mammals, like you, the system starts at the nasal cavity inside your nose. This is both the inlet and outlet for air.

Beyond this is the passageway, down the throat, which consists of the larynx and the windpipe, or trachea. These carry air down into the chest. From here the windpipe splits into two airways, called the bronchi. These carry the air into the lungs. Here, oxygen is absorbed into the blood where it can be taken to any part of your body.

LUNGS
By blowing up a balloon, you can see that air really does enter your lungs. Each breath you take pushes new air into your breathing system, which can be forced out into the balloon, causing it to inflate (below).

BEHIND THE NOSE
Filling the space between the base of the skull and the top of the jaw is the nasal cavity (see page 8). It is split in two by a single piece of cartilage.

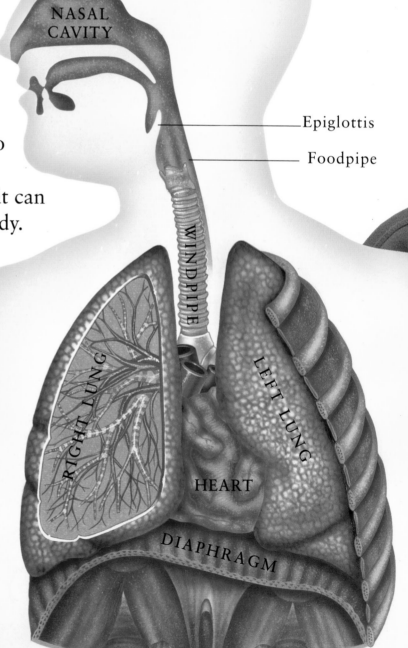

NASAL CAVITY

Epiglottis

Foodpipe

WINDPIPE

RIGHT LUNG

LEFT LUNG

HEART

DIAPHRAGM

6

NOSE AND NOSTRILS
The nose is supported by a framework of tough yet slightly flexible plates of cartilage. The openings called nostrils allow air to pass through them, in and out of the nasal cavity.

WATER LOSS
The inner lining of the respiratory system is coated with moist mucus. Water vapour continually evaporates from it into the air that you breathe out. On a cold day, you can see the warm vapour as it condenses into a "mist" of fine droplets (left).

In some diseases and injuries, the patient is not able to breathe properly. This may be due to damage to the breathing muscles, nerves or parts of the brain controlling them. Various types of medical machines called ventilators or respirators can mechanically pump air in and out of the lungs, to copy normal breathing movements (right).

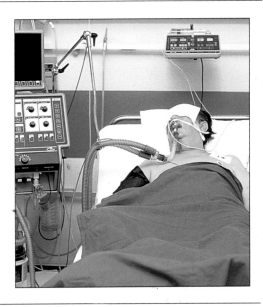

STERNUM

RIB

CHEST
The chest is also called the thorax. It forms the upper part of your main body, from the shoulders down to the large sheet of muscle called the diaphragm just beneath the lungs. Below this is the part of your body known as the abdomen.

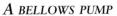

RIBCAGE
Your soft lungs are surrounded by a cage of bones, which you can see beneath your skin. The bony "bars" of this cage are your ribs. Holding these together at the front of your chest is the breast bone, or sternum (above).

A BELLOWS PUMP
The chest works rather like an old-fashioned bellows, sucking air in by expanding or increasing in size, and then blowing the air out again by becoming smaller.

EPIGLOTTIS

The epiglottis is a stiff, flap-like part found where the throat divides into the windpipe and the foodpipe. When you are breathing, it is tilted up, allowing air to pass into the windpipe and on to the lungs. During the swallowing of food or drink, the epiglottis tilts over to cover the top of the windpipe. If food were to go down the windpipe, you would choke (see page 24). Instead, it passes into the foodpipe and on to the stomach (below).

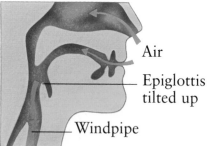

Air
Epiglottis tilted up
Windpipe

Breathing

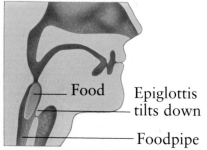

Food
Epiglottis tilts down
Foodpipe

Swallowing

ADAM'S APPLE AND WINDPIPE

You can see part of your windpipe at the top of your neck, it's called the Adam's apple (main picture). This forms part of your voice box, or larynx, which contains the vocal cords that make the sounds of your voice. The larynx, in turn, leads on to your windpipe. Below this, the tube leads down your neck (right), into your chest and down into your lungs.

NASAL CAVITY

The surface of the cavity (left) is filled with blood vessels that bring warm blood to heat the breathed-in air. The surface is also covered in a layer of fine hairs (see page 25). Finally, the cavity houses the organs that help you smell.

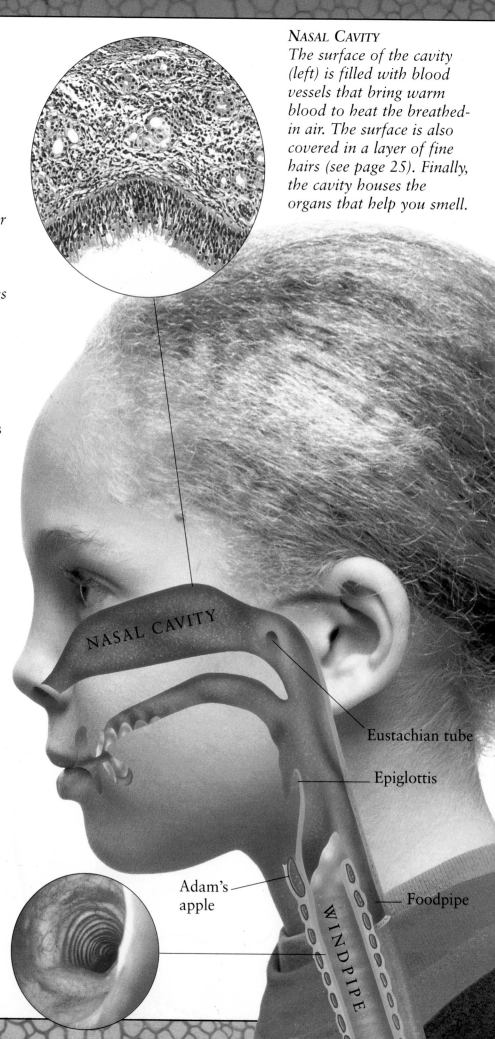

NASAL CAVITY

Eustachian tube

Epiglottis

Adam's apple

WINDPIPE

Foodpipe

8

The MOUTH, NOSE & THROAT

YOU CAN BREATHE IN AND OUT either through your nose or your mouth. However, the nose is better to breathe through as the blood-rich lining inside it warms and moistens the air before it passes into the respiratory system. The inside is coated with nasal hairs and a sticky mucus lining which filter out floating dust and other particles. This warmed, moistened and cleaned air is better suited to flow into your lungs, compared with air you may have breathed through your mouth.

Your nose also holds your smell organs which detect if there is anything nasty in the air that you may not want to breathe in.

Muscle   Cartilage

KEEPING THE WINDPIPE OPEN
Your windpipe or trachea (above) is supported by C-shaped rings of cartilage. These rings ensure that the windpipe does not collapse under the pressure of the internal organs that surround it.

9

The lining inside the nasal cavity is soft, spongy and delicate. It is richly supplied with blood vessels that warm and moisten incoming air. This is why a knock to the nose, or even a hard sneeze or nose-blow, can damage it, rupturing the vessels and causing a nose bleed. The usual treatment is to breathe through the mouth and pinch the fleshy part of the nose just below the bridge. Eventually, the blood should clot. But it is important not to knock or even blow the nose soon after, as this may start the bleeding again.

NOSE AND EARS
Two thin passages, called eustachian tubes, link the back of the nasal cavity with the air-filled chambers found inside each ear. These tubes let air pass through, to equalise changes in pressure. If you hold your nose shut, close your mouth and blow very gently, you may feel air going along the tubes into your ears. This will make your ears go "pop" (above).

The LUNGS

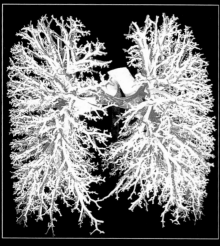

THE TWO LUNGS are like pinky-grey, cone-shaped sponges, one in either side of the chest. Between them are the heart with its main blood vessels, the windpipe bringing air to the lungs from the nose and throat, and the foodpipe, which passes down behind the trachea, to the stomach. Each lung contains amazingly intricate and interwoven networks of branching airways (above), tiny air sacs called alveoli, and blood vessels. These are all held together by a tough, elastic mixture of fibres and other substances.

BRANCHING AIRWAYS
Before it reaches the lungs, the windpipe divides into two airways, or bronchi. Once inside the lungs, these airways will divide again (right), and continue to divide into smaller tubes called bronchioles. After about 16 divisions, the airways form terminal bronchioles, which are too narrow to see with the naked eye. These airways finally end with the alveoli.

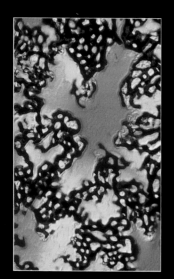

INSIDE LUNGS
Under a microscope, the lungs appear as a collection of tiny air spaces surrounded by lung tissue (left). These air spaces are the alveoli and the surrounding tissue holds the vessels that carry blood into the lungs.

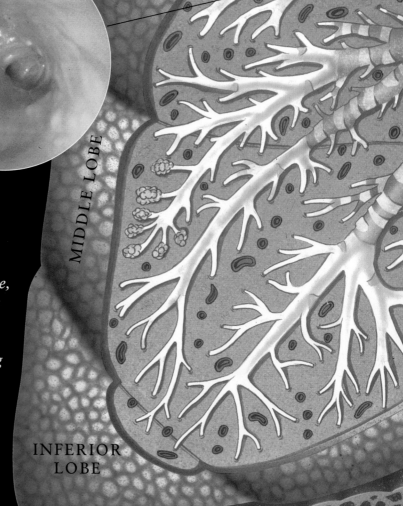

SUPERIOR LOBE

MIDDLE LOBE

INFERIOR LOBE

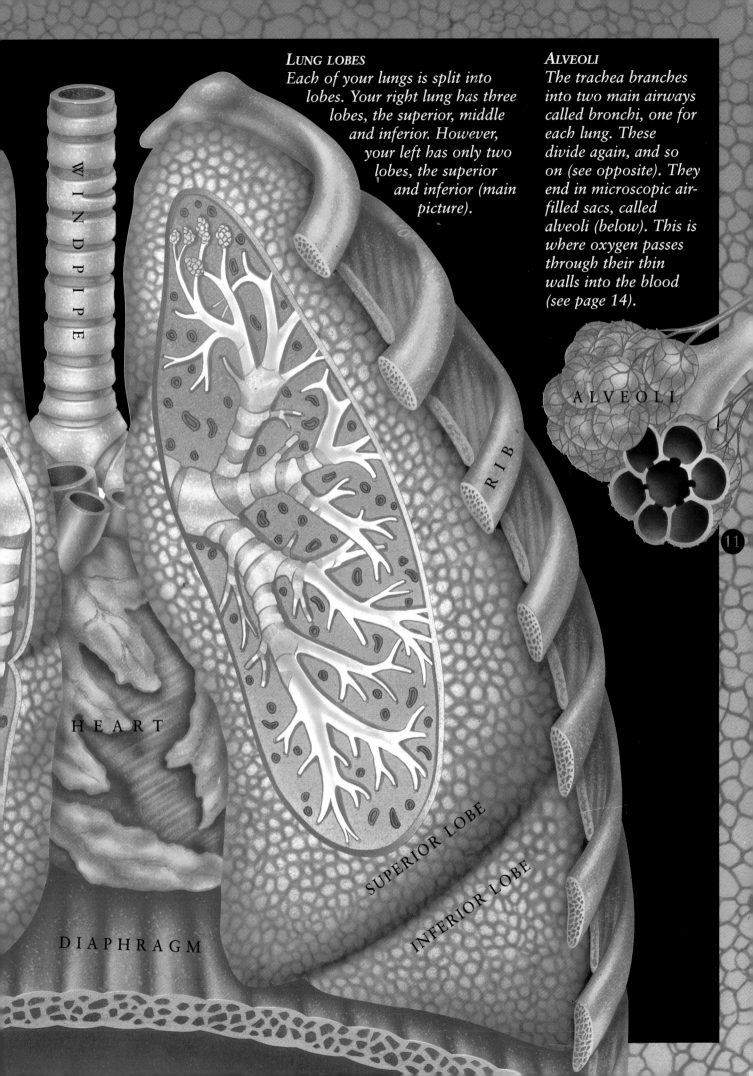

LUNG LOBES

Each of your lungs is split into lobes. Your right lung has three lobes, the superior, middle and inferior. However, your left has only two lobes, the superior and inferior (main picture).

ALVEOLI

The trachea branches into two main airways called bronchi, one for each lung. These divide again, and so on (see opposite). They end in microscopic air-filled sacs, called alveoli (below). This is where oxygen passes through their thin walls into the blood (see page 14).

ALVEOLI

W I N D P I P E

R I B

11

H E A R T

SUPERIOR LOBE

INFERIOR LOBE

D I A P H R A G M

BREATHING IN,...

BREATHING IN, also called inhalation or inspiration, is the start of the breathing process. Although you might take it for granted most of the time, this process requires some quite complicated feats of coordination by your body.

For air to enter your lungs, their size must be increased. To do this requires the movement of at least two body parts, your ribcage and your diaphragm. These must work at the same time, otherwise air would not enter your lungs and your body would be starved of oxygen.

12

UP AND DOWN RIBS
While you are breathing, you will see your ribcage rising and falling with each breath. This movement is caused by the muscles between your ribs, called the intercostals, contracting. As they contract, they pull the ribcage up and out (right). This causes the lungs inside to expand, forcing fresh air into them.

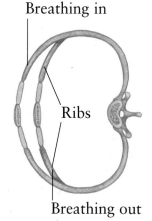

Breathing in

Ribs

Breathing out

Ribs move up and out

Intercostals

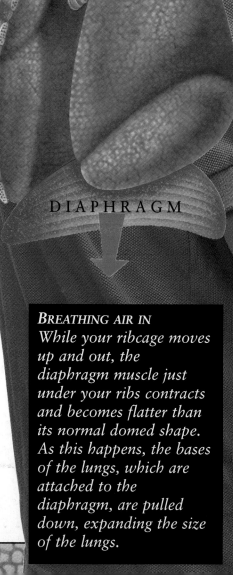

DIAPHRAGM

HOW MUCH AIR?
The total amount of air held by the lungs, after breathing in as deeply as possible, is about 6 litres (12 pints – left) for adult men and 4-5 litres (9 pints) for adult women. However, during normal quiet breathing, when the body is at rest, only about half a litre (1 pint) of air is taken in and then blown out again, with each breath.

BREATHING AIR IN
While your ribcage moves up and out, the diaphragm muscle just under your ribs contracts and becomes flatter than its normal domed shape. As this happens, the bases of the lungs, which are attached to the diaphragm, are pulled down, expanding the size of the lungs.

BREATHING OUT

ONCE AIR has entered your lungs, and gas exchange has taken place (see page 14), it is time to breathe out, also called exhalation or expiration. If this did not take place then carbon dioxide levels would build up in your body, which would be fatal.

To get rid of this "used" air, the diaphragm and the muscles between the ribs simply relax. This decreases the size of the lungs and pushes the air out.

Ribs move down and in

DIAPHRAGM

HELPING BREATHING
People with breathing problems are encouraged to sit up rather than lie down (right). This stops the stomach and other organs from pressing on the diaphragm, which can make breathing more difficult.

The short, noisy inhalations known as hiccups are caused by uncontrollable contractions, called spasms, of the diaphragm. Each one sucks in air unexpectedly, causing the epiglottis to snap shut. Hiccups have many causes. One is eating or drinking too quickly, which stretches the stomach and presses on the diaphragm. This can irritate either the diaphragm or the nerves leading to it, which carry nerve signals telling it when to contract. Another cause is a sudden fright. Cures for hiccups include sipping water very slowly and holding your breath.

BLOWING AIR OUT
Normal breathing out is a passive process, involving the relaxing of your intercostals and diaphragm. If you wish to force air out, then other muscles must be used, such as your abdominal muscles. These contract, squeezing on the chest and making your lungs smaller.

13

OXYGEN IN, CARBON DIOXIDE OUT

AS YOUR BODY "burns" fuel and oxygen to create the energy it needs to stay alive, it makes the waste product carbon dioxide. This is poisonous to the body and has to be removed. Your blood system carries this waste product to the lungs where it seeps into the alveoli in the lungs and is breathed out (see page 13).

At the same time, oxygen seeps from the air in the lungs into the blood system and it is carried to your body's cells where it can be used to create more energy. This swapping of gasses between the air in the lungs and the blood system is called the gas exchange.

RESPIRATION AND COMBUSTION

Energy production has been likened to a slow, continuous fire burning inside your body (below). Like a fire, energy production needs both fuel and oxygen to work. Its fuel comes from the food you eat, which your body breaks down into simple parts, such as sugars.

Then, just as a fire produces smoke and other gases, your body's energy production makes waste products, such as carbon dioxide.

Carries Oxygen

Carries Carbon Dioxide

GAS EXCHANGE: PART 1

Each alveolus is wrapped in a mesh of tiny blood vessels, called capillaries. The walls of each alveolus and capillary are only one cell thick. This lets the two gases seep through them quickly (left). As this happens, the blood changes colour, from a deep reddy-blue when it has lots of carbon dioxide, to a bright red when it has lots of oxygen.

OXYGEN

ALVEOLUS

CARBON DIOXIDE

RED BLOOD CELLS

Heart

it is pumped at great pressure to all parts of the body (main picture). As it flows into the narrow blood vessels called capillaries, oxygen seeps from the blood into the surrounding body cells (left). In return, carbon dioxide, which the cells have produced while making energy, seeps into the blood. From here it travels back to the heart and then the lungs, where it is breathed out.

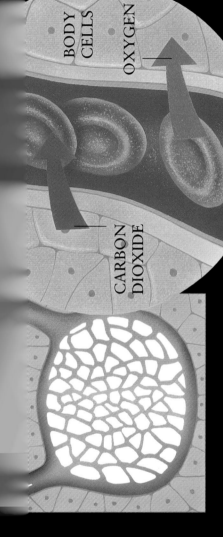

BODY CELLS

OXYGEN

CARBON DIOXIDE

IN THE BODY CELLS

Once out of the blood system, the oxygen is absorbed by each of the body's cells (below). Once inside the cell it is used to break apart the sugars that you have eaten. This process releases energy which the cell can use to divide or grow. Another product of this process is carbon dioxide, which the body must get rid of.

GAS CARRIER

Blood is an amazing liquid. Its main ingredients are millions of tiny red blood cells (right) which float in a watery liquid called plasma. The red blood cells carry oxygen from the lungs, and take carbon dioxide away from the tissues around the body.

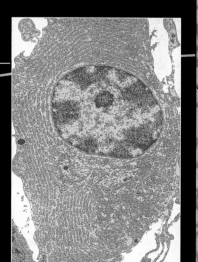

RATES OF BREATHING

T HE RATE OF BREATHING is controlled by parts of the brain (see page 18). It is adjusted to suit the needs of the body in different situations.

Internal body processes such as keeping cells alive, digestion and maintaining body temperature use small and fairly continuous amounts of energy and oxygen. Much greater amounts are needed when the body is moving rapidly, playing sports or doing other strenuous activities which require large muscle movements.

This is why you breathe faster and deeper when you exercise, as it lets you take more air into your lungs where your body can absorb more oxygen.

REACHING THE LIMIT
As the body works harder and harder, there comes a point where your breathing system can no longer keep up with oxygen demand or carbon dioxide removal. Your body will then rapidly tire, and if it is not rested immediately you could collapse with exhaustion (above) or even fall into a coma.

T here are various explanations for a "stitch" – the mysterious sharp, needle-like pain that occurs on the side of your body (left). One explanation of this is the diaphragm is not receiving enough oxygen. Before long the diaphragm will tire and be unable to contract, causing the stitch.

This most commonly occurs when you exercise shortly after eating food. As you eat, blood is diverted to your digestive system and away from the other muscles of the body, including the diaphragm. Should you then start to exercise soon after the meal, the diaphragm will not have enough oxygen to maintain its contractions, before tiring.

EXTRA OXYGEN
Normal air is about 21 per cent oxygen (see page 22). This limits the amount of oxygen which the respiratory system can absorb. If needed, people can breathe pure oxygen using a face mask and cylinder (right).

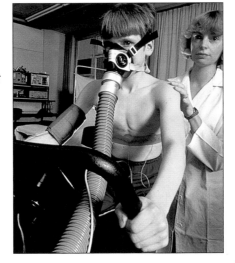

AEROBIC AND ANAEROBIC
Your body's cells are able to produce energy without using oxygen. This is called anaerobic respiration. However, it can only maintain this for activities over short periods of time, such as weight-training (below). For more extended activities, like walking (below), your body will use aerobic respiration, which does require oxygen.

DURING EXERCISE
As you start to exercise, your breathing will become deeper and the rate will increase to almost 50-60 times a minute, in order to get more oxygen into your body. However, for extremes of activity, the breathing rate continues to rise but the depth reduces, giving short, fast, shallow panting.

At the same time your heart will start to beat faster and stronger. This pushes the blood through the system faster, allowing it to carry more oxygen to the body's cells and carry carbon dioxide away.

AT REST
Breathing is usually slowest and shallowest when the body is at rest (right) or asleep. At this time, only the essential muscles are at work, These include a few muscles to hold your body position, those involved in digestion and the breathing muscles.

Average breathing rates at rest vary with age. A new baby will breathe 40-50 times a minute, a four-year-old child 25 times a minute, while an adult will only breathe 12-18 times a minute.

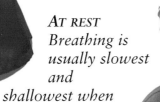

HOW MUCH AIR?
In an average day, with periods of rest, mild activity and a few bursts of action, the average person breathes in and out up to 13,000 litres (3,000 gallons) of air. This would fill about 50,000 drink cans!

17

RESPIRATORY CENTRE

Several areas of the brain stem (below), work together to control breathing rate. Some parts of the brain stem will tell the breathing muscles to contract, then to relax. Other areas make breathing deeper, as levels of carbon dioxide rise and oxygen fall in the blood.

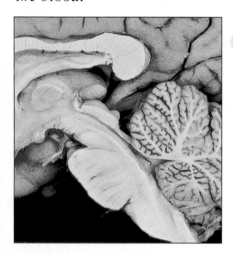

SENSING GASES

Special sensors detect the levels of oxygen and carbon dioxide in the blood. They are found in the brain and in some of the arteries, such as the aorta above the heart and the carotid arteries in the neck (right).

TISSUE SENSORS

Your lungs contain thousands of tiny sensors, that are found throughout the airways. They can detect and tell your brain whether your lungs are taking in too much air and in danger of becoming damaged.

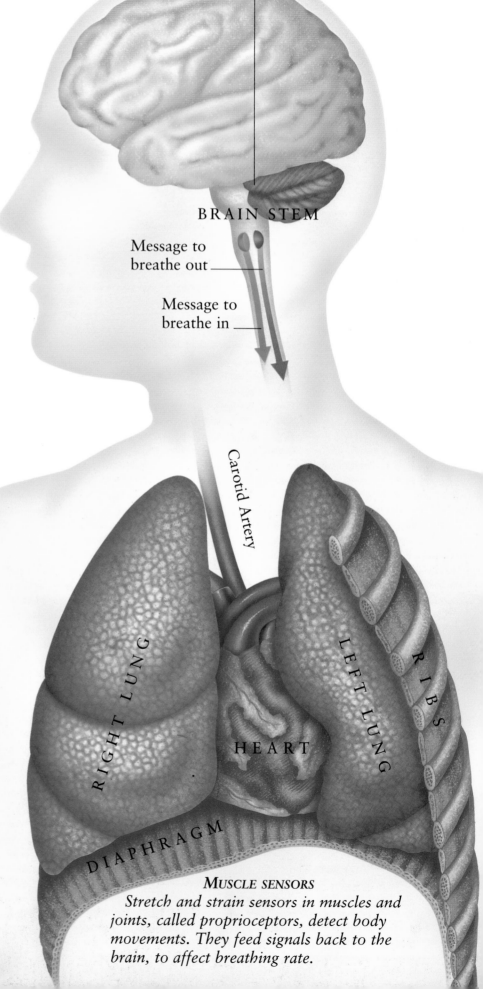

BRAIN STEM

Message to breathe out

Message to breathe in

Carotid Artery

RIGHT LUNG

LEFT LUNG

RIBS

HEART

DIAPHRAGM

MUSCLE SENSORS

Stretch and strain sensors in muscles and joints, called proprioceptors, detect body movements. They feed signals back to the brain, to affect breathing rate.

BREATHING CONTROL

How does your body know when its oxygen intake is running low, and it needs to take in more air? Control of breathing is based in the brain. It gathers information from a number of sensors around the body which continuously monitor different processes and levels. These include how much the body is moving as well as the levels of various gases, such as oxygen and carbon dioxide, in the blood.

These sensors then feed their information to the brain, through the network of nerves. The brain then analyses this information, and sends signals out to control the breathing muscles.

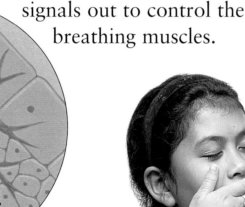

FREE NERVE ENDINGS

THE CONTROL CENTRE
Like the control centre of a space mission (below), the brain runs almost every process inside the body. However, just as your breathing takes place most of the time without you being aware of it, so most of your bodily activities are performed unconsciously. These include digesting your food and making your heart beat.

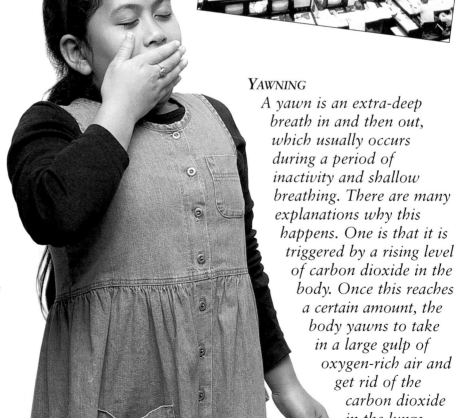

NERVE ENDINGS
Certain sensors in the skin, such as the free nerve endings (above), detect pain or heat. A sudden, unexpected pain sensation, such as picking up a hot plate, will cause an instinctive sharp intake of breath, or gasp. This intake of oxygen prepares the person for any sudden movements that might be needed to remove them from the source of the pain, i.e. drop the plate.

YAWNING
A yawn is an extra-deep breath in and then out, which usually occurs during a period of inactivity and shallow breathing. There are many explanations why this happens. One is that it is triggered by a rising level of carbon dioxide in the body. Once this reaches a certain amount, the body yawns to take in a large gulp of oxygen-rich air and get rid of the carbon dioxide in the lungs.

Epiglottis

Vocal cords

Adam's apple

Plates of cartilage

Windpipe

THE VOICE BOX
The voice box, or larynx, forms the top part of your windpipe. It consists of a box-like framework made from stiff plates of firm gristle, or cartilage (left). It sticks out a little from your neck, forming your Adam's apple (see page 8). Inside it houses the epiglottis as well as the equipment that is necessary to create your voice – your vocal cords (see below).

VOCAL CORDS
These tough, pale, shelf-like folds of tissue are responsible for making the sounds of your voice. As air is pushed from your lungs, it passes up your windpipe and through the narrow gap between the vocal cords, called the glottis. Normally this is quite wide and air can pass through easily. But, when the cords have been pulled together by muscles in the voice box, then the passing air causes the cords to vibrate, making a sound (below).

Closed for speech

Open for breathing

MOUTH AND TONGUE SHAPE SOUNDS

Epiglottis

Foodpipe

Vocal cords vibrate

Windpipe

Air from lungs

MAKING A NOISE

THE MANY SOUNDS of human speech, from whispering to talking and shouting, and also noises such as giggles, laughter, sobs and screams, are called vocalizations. These are formed by your vocal cords vibrating and creating sounds.

Your voice, and the sounds you make, depend on a number of things. For example, a man's voice is low in pitch because the vocal cords in a man are larger and less taut than those in a woman. The volume of sound you make is dependent on the speed that air is forced up through your voice box. Your voice is also affected by the shape of the air passages in your head, and finally by the positions of your lips, tongue and teeth, which can be moved to form words when you are speaking.

THE VIBRATING REED
The reed in a reed-based musical instrument, such as the saxophone (above), works in the same way as the vocal cords. It vibrates in a stream of moving air to make sounds. These are amplified and altered by the rest of the instrument, in the same way that the human voice is altered by the throat, mouth, nose and sinuses.

21

SINUSES
The sinuses are air-filled chambers found within the skull bones around the back of the eyes and above the nose. These are connected to the main nasal cavity by small, internal openings. Along with the other air passages in the throat and mouth, these cavities work like echo chambers. Together, they make the sounds from the vocal cords louder and help to give your voice its distinctive sound.

SINUSES

LOUD AND QUIET
Your voice can go from a quiet whisper to a loud yell (above). However, if you shout too much your voice may become hoarse. This is caused by your vocal cords swelling and not being able to close properly. As a result air leaks between the cords, causing the hoarseness.

A BREATH OF FRESH AIR

No other planet in the solar system has an atmosphere like the Earth. It plays an essential role in supporting life on the planet, providing the gases that are needed to produce energy for life, as well as the climate that makes life bearable.

However, as cities all over the world have expanded, and advances in technology have led to the production of more machines, so pollution levels have risen. Today the air on city streets contains much more than just fresh air. It is filled with a cocktail of chemicals. These chemicals pollute the atmosphere, creating conditions that may be harmful to you and to other living things.

CITY AIR
A face mask can be used to filter out the polluted air on city streets. This is especially helpful when the lungs are working hard, such as when cycling (above).

SMOG
Smog is caused by polluting gases, such as sulphurous and nitrous oxides, and tiny floating particles given off by all kinds of machines, especially those which burn fossil fuels, such as heaters and diesel trucks. Usually, this pollution spreads up and out and gets dispersed by the wind. But in some cities, such as Milan (above left), temperature and weather conditions prevent smog from being dispersed. It stays close to the ground as a thick, choking haze.

NITROGEN
The majority of air is made up of the gas, nitrogen, forming 79 per cent of the atmosphere. However, it is of little use to your body.

22

Other gases

About a dozen gases make up a tiny fraction of normal air. They include carbon dioxide (0.04 per cent), neon (0.0018 per cent) and helium (0.0005 per cent).

Argon

Argon forms just under one per cent of air. It is one of a group of chemicals, called the noble gases, which means it takes place in few chemical changes.

Oxygen

This gas forms about 20 per cent of fresh air. After breathing the air in, some of the oxygen is absorbed by the lungs, so exhaled air contains only about 16 per cent.

Carbon monoxide

Vehicle exhausts (right) contain a gas called carbon monoxide. This is very poisonous to the body because the red cells in blood prefer to attach to it, rather than to oxygen (see page 15). Before long, carbon monoxide replaces oxygen in the blood, poisoning the person.

The atmosphere

The layer of air closest to the Earth is called the troposphere (right), which stretches to a height of between 10 to 15 km (6 to 9 miles). This region supports all the life on the planet and is responsible for most of the weather. Above this, air starts to thin rapidly as the atmosphere enters the stratosphere, which stretches up to about 50 km (31 miles). As it reaches into space, the atmosphere dwindles away, and astronauts need special protective equipment to survive (above).

OZONE LAYER

STRATOSPHERE

TROPOSPHERE

PROTECTIVE CLOTHING

The lungs are not able to get rid of all the particles that may be breathed in. Some, such as asbestos, may stay in the lungs and cause cancer. When handling asbestos, it is important to wear special clothing, including a face mask (left).

MUCUS

Most of your air passages are lined with a layer of mucus. This acts as a barrier, coating the delicate tissue layer beneath and preventing any dirt particles from irritating it. The mucus is constantly made by tiny glands and goblet cells found in the walls of the breathing system (below).

CILIA HAIRS

DIRT

MUCUS GLAND

GOBLET CELL

CILIA HAIRS

Your windpipe and upper airways are lined with microscopic hairs called cilia (right). These beat, or wave, to and fro in a coordinated fashion, like rows of tiny oars. This "rowing" action moves the mucus layer along, like a conveyor belt. As the mucus is moved, it carries the bits of dirt and debris that have have been breathed in and become trapped in it. These foreign bodies can then be removed by either coughing them out, or swallowing them into the stomach.

Occasionally, the windpipe gets blocked and stops a person's breathing. This may happen if they try to eat and talk at the same time. The first natural reaction is to cough out the blockage. If this fails, a practised first-aider may squeeze the person's abdomen from behind, an action called the Heimlich manoeuvre (left). This may blow the blockage out.

CLEANING THE SYSTEM

A S THEY ARE in continual contact with the outside air, the lungs and all of the breathing passageways are in constant danger from many risks, such as pollution (see pages 22-23). The air you breathe in and out is almost certain to contain at least some tiny floating particles, including pollutants, dust, dirt, fragments of animal fur, bits of bird feathers and insect wings, plant pollen, fungal spores and microbes such as bacteria and viruses.

To combat this constant threat, the breathing system has several methods of defending itself against these foreign objects and removing them from your body. These objects are either expelled back out into the air, swallowed into the stomach where they are destroyed by powerful acids, or destroyed by your body's own microscopic army.

NASAL HAIRS
The hairs at the entrance to the nasal cavity help to filter out large airborne particles, such as pieces of dust and ash (above). Other bits of debris stick to the mucus lining inside the nasal cavity, which is then blown out or sniffed in.

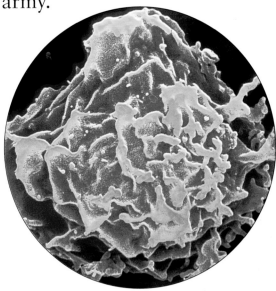

SNEEZING AND COUGHING
These natural reflex actions get rid of dust and irritating items which may block your airways. Both involve breathing in deeply, then closing the mouth or throat, as the abdominal muscles press on the lungs and force the air up the windpipe. In a sneeze, the rear of the mouth is opened and the air blasts out through the nose, dislodging particles and mucus found there and blowing them out. In a cough it blasts up the windpipe and lower throat, rattling the vocal cords and making the "hacking" noise.

MACROPHAGES
These microscopic cells (above) are a type of blood cell and part of the body's army against infection. They wander through your blood vessels and ooze out into the surrounding tissues, looking for germs and tiny fragments of debris. Once found, the macrophage will surround the foreign body and "eat" it whole.

25

SHORT OF BREATH?

DESPITE THEIR DEFENCES and cleaning systems, the lungs and breathing airways sometimes suffer problems. This may be due to prolonged exposure to harmful substances, such as smoking or mining (left) or a sudden reaction to certain things. In some people, the breathing system is extra-sensitive to normally harmless substances and reacts by becoming red and swollen. This sometimes violent reaction is termed an allergy or hypersensitivity. Hay fever is caused by an allergy to certain types of pollen grains (right). During the summer months, when pollen counts are high, these tiny grains can irritate the eyes, nose and throat.

SMOKING

Inhaling tobacco smoke has many bad effects on the airways and lungs. The smoke contains tar vapours, which form sticky blobs which clog the air passages and kill cilia hairs. Smoke also contains carbon monoxide, which lessens the ability of the blood to carry oxygen (see page 23). It also contains various cancer-causing substances.

CYSTIC FIBROSIS

This disease, which may be passed down from parent to child, affects various glands, including those which make mucus that lines the airways. The mucus is unusually thick and sticky and blocks the airways. If left untreated, it can cause chest infections and lung damage. Treatment includes draining the mucus by physiotherapy and special body postures (right).

ASTHMA

This is an allergic response, which causes the air passages to contract and their linings to swell, narrowing the airway (right), making breathing difficult, if not impossible. If treatment is not applied a severe asthma attack could prove fatal. The commonest form of treatment is with an inhaler (left), which delivers an amount of drugs that will reduce the constriction.

NORMAL AIRWAY

NARROWED AIRWAY

CAUSES OF ASTHMA

Dust mites (below) are a common cause of asthma. These microscopic creatures are very common in house dust, furniture and bedding. Their dry, powdery droppings float in the air, where they are breathed in and trigger the allergic reaction of asthma.

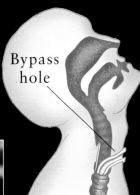

Bypass hole

A blockage in the upper breathing passages of the nose, throat and voice box, may stop air reaching the lungs. This can be very dangerous and even fatal. The blockage may be an inhaled object or liquid, severe swelling in the throat region due to a disease such as diphtheria, or an intense allergic reaction, such as to a bee sting. One emergency treatment is a tracheotomy. This involves making a bypass hole in the neck, through to the windpipe, so air can flow (above).

27

RESPIRATORY GERMS

If they are not checked, dozens of germs can infect the breathing system. They may go on to cause diseases ranging from rhinitis and the common cold to laryngitis, bronchitis and pneumonia. The influenza, or flu, virus (right) begins by infecting the airways, but soon spreads around the body, causing symptoms like headaches. The worst outbreak of influenza occured just after World War One, in the years 1918 and 1919. During this time nearly 20 million people died of the virus, more than were killed in the war itself.

The LUNGS THROUGH LIFE

T HE HUMAN BODY starts its life by not needing its lungs at all. Although they are fairly well developed, the unborn baby's lungs contain no air and cannot be used to breathe. Instead, he or she has to rely on its mother for supplies of oxygen and nutrients.

Once born, dramatic changes occur, allowing the child to breathe air. These changes continue throughout the child's life, as its lungs continue to grow into maturity and then decline when he or she reaches old age.

IN THE WOMB
During the nine months of the pregnancy, the baby spends its time in the womb submerged in a watery environment, neither breathing or eating (left). However, towards the end of this time, the baby may "practise" swallowing and breathing movements.

28

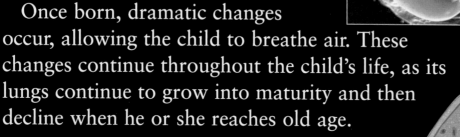

Mother's blood   Baby's blood   Umbilical Cord

PLACENTA

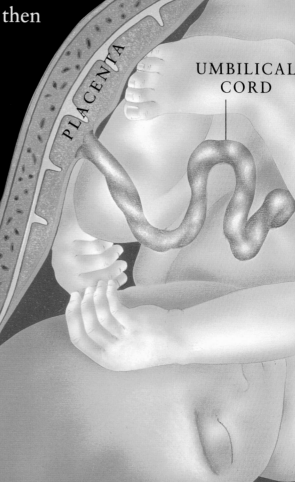

PLACENTA

UMBILICAL CORD

PLACENTA AND UMBILICAL CORD
The baby's blood passes down the twisting umbilical cord and into the placenta, which connects the baby to its mother. Here the baby's blood flows past pools of the mother's blood. The two blood systems are very close, but do not mix. Instead, oxygen and nutrients pass through the narrow divide, from the mother's blood to the baby's, while carbon dioxide and wastes go the opposite way (above). The baby's blood, now rich in oxygen, flows back along the umbilical cord.

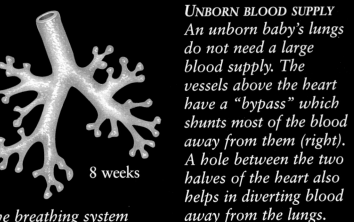

4 weeks

5 weeks

8 weeks

DEVELOPING LUNGS
Like many body parts, the breathing system develops its basic form in the unborn baby very quickly. The lungs first appear as simple branches from the windpipe about four weeks after the baby begins to grow (above). These branches become more and more numerous as the airways continue to divide. After about 24 weeks, the tiny alveoli form. By the time it is born, the baby will have only 15 per cent of the alveoli that an adult has. However, these grow in size and number until the child is eight years old.

UNBORN BLOOD SUPPLY
An unborn baby's lungs do not need a large blood supply. The vessels above the heart have a "bypass" which shunts most of the blood away from them (right). A hole between the two halves of the heart also helps in diverting blood away from the lungs. Within minutes of birth, both the hole and the tube begin to close up.

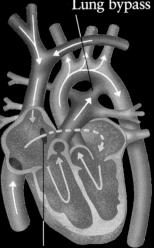

Lung bypass

Hole in heart

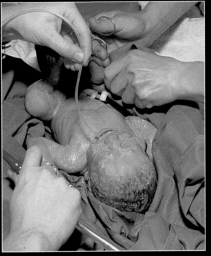

FIRST BREATHS
As a new baby emerges into the fresh air, breathing movements will open the airways (left). A natural chemical, called surfactant, helps the alveoli to inflate. All this may be helped by pats on the back and cries from the baby.

29

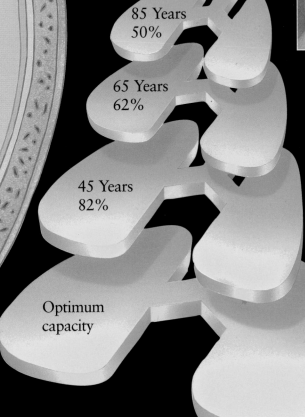

85 Years 50%

65 Years 62%

45 Years 82%

Optimum capacity

AGEING LUNGS
With increasing age, many factors reduce the ability of the lungs to absorb oxygen. This happens to the extent that by the time you reach 85 you will only be able to absorb 50 per cent of the oxygen you did 60 years before (left). One reason is that the breathing muscles become weaker with age. Also, as a result of the many micro-injuries which are part of daily life, scar tissue grows in the lungs. This tissue starts to fill airways and alveoli, making the lungs fibrous in appearance (above).

KNOW YOUR BODY

Pearl divers in the South Pacific can stay underwater for nearly two and a half minutes (above). The greatest depth to which a human has dived without the help of breathing apparatus is 107 m (351 ft) by the Italian Angela Bandini who was underwater for 2 min 46 sec. In comparison, Sperm whales (below) can dive to over 3,000 m (9,840 ft) below the surface, in dives that last for nearly 2 hours!

Each tiny alveoli is only 25 micrometres (1/1,000 inch) across. However, there are 700 million of them in both of your lungs. If they were flattened out into one sheet, they would cover an area roughly equivalent to a tennis court (right).

Because your heart sits on the left side of your body, your left lung is slightly smaller than your right lung (left). In fact, the right lung of an adult weighs about 700 g (21 ounces) and the left roughly 650 g (20 ounces).

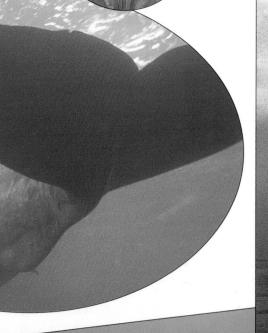

The loudest noise made by a human voice was by the Australian Simon Robinson, who screamed at an astonishing 128 decibels. In comparison, the jet engine on an aeroplane makes about 130 decibels (right).

Your sneezes can throw stuff out of your nose at amazing speeds. Air can leave your nose at an astonishing 160 km/h (100 mph), only slightly less than the winds in a tornado, which can reach up to 180 km/h (112 mph) (above).

GLOSSARY

Aerobic respiration – The production of energy that involves oxygen.

Alveoli – The tiny, bubble-like units found at the ends of the bronchioles. It is here that gas exchange takes place.

Anaerobic respiration – The production of energy that does not involve the use of oxygen.

Brain stem – The stalk of the brain which controls the rate of breathing.

Bronchi – The branches of the windpipe that lead into the lungs.

Bronchioles – Small tubes that branch from the bronchi and continue to branch until they end with the alveoli.

Cartilage – Also called "gristle", this tough tissue provides support to certain organs in the body.

Chlorophyll – A green chemical found in all green parts of a plant. It traps sunlight for use in photosynthesis.

Cilia – Short, hair-like projections lining the airways. These move to and fro in a "rowing" action to help remove dirt from the breathing system.

Diffusion – The "seeping" movement of a gas or liquid from an area of high concentration to an area of low concentration.

Epiglottis – A flap of cartilage that covers the opening to the windpipe while swallowing food. This prevents choking.

Eustachian tubes – Two small tubes that lead from the back of the mouth to each ear.

Exhale – Forcing air out of the lungs by relaxing the diaphragm and letting the ribcage fall.

Gills – The organs in the fish that absorb oxygen from the water.

Inhale – An intake of breath which involves expanding the lungs to force air into them.

Intercostal muscles – The muscles found between the ribs which contract to lift the ribcage.

Larynx – Also called the voice box, this small tube contains the vocal cords. It is situated at the base of the throat.

Lungs – A pair of organs that are the sites of oxygen absorption. They are found in the chest.

Macrophage – A type of blood cell that is part of the body's immune system. It "eats" objects that are foreign to the body, such as debris and bacteria.

Photosynthesis – The production of food by green plants using water, carbon dioxide and light energy from the sun.

Placenta – An organ filled with blood vessels that provides the link between the unborn baby and its mother. Oxygen and nutrients pass through it to nourish the baby.

Respiration – The overall exchange of oxygen and carbon dioxide between the atmosphere, lungs, blood and body cells.

Sinus – An air space found in the skull. It aids in sound production and makes the skull lighter.

Spiracle – An opening on an insect's skin that lets air into its breathing system.

Trachea – Also called the windpipe, this tube leads from the top of the neck, below the voice box, down towards the lungs.

Umbilical cord – A tube, connecting the unborn baby and the placenta.

INDEX

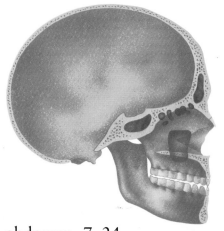

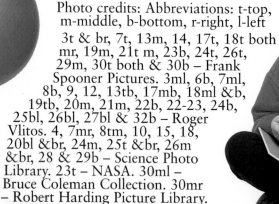